ENGINEERING EVOLUTIONS

Transportation

From the Earliest Journeys to High-Tech Travel

SARAH EASON AND CATHLEEN SMALL

CHERITON
CHILDREN'S BOOKS

Published in 2026 by Cheriton Children's Books
1 Bank Drive West, Shrewsbury, Shropshire, SY3 9DJ, UK

First Edition

Authors: Sarah Eason and Cathleen Small
Editor: Jennifer Sanderson
Designer: Paul Myerscough
Proofreader: Ellie Truman

Picture credits: Cover: Shutterstock/Peter Fleming (left), Shutterstock/Ta2ng Ko (right). Inside: p1: Shutterstock/Bjoern Wylezich, p4: Shutterstock/Synthetic Messiah, p5: Shutterstock/Suwin66, p6: Shutterstock/Gorodenkoff, p7: Shutterstock/WR Studio, p8: Shutterstock/Viacheslav Lopatin, p9: Shutterstock/AI Generator, p10: Wikimedia Commons/Edward Keble Chatterton, p11: Shutterstock/PairutPanyamano, p12: Shutterstock/NeagoneFo, p13: Shutterstock/Alex Segre, p14t: Shutterstock/Viktor Hladchenko, p14b: Shutterstock/Jose Mario Espinoza, p15: Shutterstock/Jdross75, p16: Shutterstock/HodagMedia, p17: Shutterstock/Ryan Fletcher, p18t: Wikimedia Commons/Claude Louis Desrais, p18b: Shutterstock/Everett Collection, p20: Shutterstock/John Selway, p21: Shutterstock/ATEF MS80, p22: Shutterstock/Kichigin, p23: Shutterstock/Gabriel Nica, p24: Shutterstock/Andriy Baidak, p25: Shutterstock/Santi Rodriguez, p26: Shutterstock/Takashi Images, p27: Shutterstock/Scharfsinn, p29t: Shutterstock/AlinStock, p29b: Shutterstock/Tada Images, p30: Shutterstock/CTR Photos, p31: Shutterstock/Kardasov Films, p32: Shutterstock/Cyo Bo, p33: Shutterstock/IamDoctorEgg, p34: Shutterstock/Stefan Holm, p35: Shutterstock/Bjoern Wylezich, p36: Shutterstock/Anatoliy Gleb, p37: Shutterstock/Alexander Mogilevets, p38: Shutterstock/Mislik, p39: Shutterstock/Gorodenkoff, p40: Shutterstock/Mike Fuchslocher, p41: Shutterstock/Aapsky, p42: Shutterstock/No-Mad, p43: Shutterstock/PeopleImages.com/Yuri A, p44: Shutterstock/Arnold OA Pinto, p45: Shutterstock/Aerogondo2, p46: Wikimedia Commons/Erik Christensen, p47: Shutterstock/Goncharovaia, p48: Wikimedia Commons/Margauux P, p49: Shutterstock/Bjoern Wylezich, p50: Roboat/MIT/AMS Institute, p51: Shutterstock/Boligolov Andrew, p52: Shutterstock/AU USAnakul, p53: Shutterstock/Frantic00, p54: Shutterstock/CC7, p55: Shutterstock/Matyas Rehak, p56: Shutterstock/Wosunan, p57: Shutterstock/Gorodenkoff, p58: Shutterstock/PitukTV.

Printed in China

CONTENTS

EVOLUTIONS IN ENGINEERING

Engineering is the use of scientific, mathematical, and practical ideas to design and create things such as vehicles, machines, and devices. Those things solve problems and improve people's lives. The people who come up with these ideas are engineers. We have engineers to thank for the many innovations in transportation that have happened across the ages. They are responsible for the evolution in transportation throughout history, from the invention of the wheel to flying on jet airplanes and driving electric vehicles. They have made modern transportation possible.

What Is Transportation?

Transportation is the moving of people, animals, or objects from one place to another. There are a lot of different ways that things are transported. When it comes to people and things we need to move around, we most often use land, air, and water transportation. These are the three key parts of transportation:

1. **Infrastructure:** This includes the facilities and systems needed for transportation, such as roads, airports, and waterways.
2. **Vehicles:** From planes and trains to bicycles and cars, there are many different machines that move things from place to place.
3. **Operations:** These are the things that make transportation possible. For example, air traffic control systems must be in place to make air travel safe and efficient.

Travel by airplane makes it easy and quick to move around the world.

Finding Solutions

Transportation has helped us travel across our world. It has improved our lives, by making it easier to move the goods we need from one place to another. However, using machines to transport things has created problems. For example, vehicles give off harmful emissions that contribute to global warming. More and more roads are being built to carry the ever-increasing number of vehicles. However, these roads harm the environment in many ways. We need the shipping industry, which helps us transport goods across water, to and from countries. However, powering these ships also has a harmful impact on the environment. And as engineers try to find even faster ways to transport people and goods from one place to another, they need to understand the environmental issues these new means of transportation bring. Can the engineers of today and tomorrow find solutions to these many challenges?

Perhaps one day travel across cities will be by self-driving air taxis!

An Engineering Evolution

In this book, we'll explore great feats of engineering in transportation throughout history, from earliest times to the present day. We'll discover how engineering has evolved and how ancient engineering has inspired modern engineering. We'll learn how engineers have come up with resourceful ways to solve the transportation issues people face today. We'll also explore the exciting developments in engineering that are just around the corner for the transportation industry. And we'll discover how they could provide the answer to our future growing transportation needs.

CHAPTER 1

THE HISTORY OF TRANSPORTATION

Early man had only one option for getting around: by foot.

In the early days of human history, transportation was simple: people walked. Early humans were nomadic. This means they traveled around and did not live in one place. They hunted and gathered food to feed themselves and those in their community. They tracked and hunted the animals they ate by following them on foot from place to place. However, traveling on foot was difficult when trying to cross large areas of water, such as rivers. It was also hard on land, as people often needed to carry heavy loads across distances. So they came up with smart ways to get over these issues: using animals and making vehicles.

Traveling Across Water

To move more easily across water, people built boats and rafts. Some rafts were made of wood, such as bamboo or reeds that were bound together. People also used bound reeds and logs as rafts. Pieces of wood that floated on the water became simple rafts. The first boats were similar to canoes and were known as logboats or dugouts. These boats were hollowed-out trees. One of the earliest known logboats is the Pesse canoe. It was uncovered in the Netherlands, Europe, in 1955 during the building of a road. Scientists believe that the boat was built somewhere between 8040 and 7510 BCE.

ENGINEERING EVOLUTIONS

Discover how water travel has evolved from ancient times to today in chapter 4.

Using Animals and Building Machines

Around 12000 BCE, people stopped being nomadic and began farming. Around 4000 BCE, they started to keep large animals such as horses and cattle. It is likely that they used these animals to help them transport heavy loads across distances. The next step was to create machines to help them transport things across land. By about 8000 BCE, people in northern Europe were using sleds to help them move things across snow and ice. And by the time of ancient Egypt (3100–30 BCE), people were using sleds to move loads across dry land.

BIG Breakthroughs

By far one of the biggest of all breakthroughs in transportation has to be the invention of the wheel. The wheel is one of the most important engineering inventions of all time. Wheels made transportation much more efficient. Experts argue about when the wheel was invented, but it is generally thought to have been somewhere around 4000 BCE.

By 3500 BCE, wheeled vehicles such as carts were used by several civilizations, including the Mesopotamians. This exciting new method of transportation allowed people to move at faster speeds over greater distances. It also paved the way for later wheeled inventions, including the modern automobile.

This model illustrates an early human fishing boat.

ENGINEERING EVOLUTIONS

Discover how wheeled transportation has evolved from ancient times to today in chapter 2.

This carving shows an ancient Egyptian chariot.

New and Improved Wheels

By around 2000 BCE, the spoked wheel had been invented in Anatolia (now modern-day Turkey). A spoke is a rod that reaches from the center of a wheel to its edge. Before the invention of spokes, wheels were solid and heavy. Spokes made the wheels much lighter. That meant vehicles could move more quickly. Spoked wheels paved the way for faster transportation of goods between areas. They also allowed people to create fast-moving vehicles such as chariots, which were used in battles. Chariots were used by many ancient civilizations. They included the ancient Egyptians, Hittites, and ancient Chinese.

BIG Breakthroughs

The Romans were great engineers who revolutionized transportation. They created stronger, straighter, and longer roads than ever before seen. Roman engineers designed roads that had layers. The bottom layer was broken stones. Next was a layer of medium-to-large stones. Then came a layer of gravel mixed with cement. On top of that layer was sand mixed with cement. Finally, the top layer was made of flat, wide stones. Roman roads also had a slight camber. That means they sloped downward from the center on either side. That allowed water to run off the road onto surrounding land. Roman roads were so well built that many of them have survived since ancient times.

One of the first great Roman roads was named the Via Appia. It was built in 312 BCE. It ran southeast from Rome to Brindisi, on the southern coast of Italy. It covered 162 miles (261 km). The Romans built a great network of similar roads across their empire. That helped them control huge areas of the world, from the Mediterranean to Britain and other parts of northern Europe. All in all, the Romans built around 50,000 miles (80,000 km) of roads, which they mainly used to move their army from one area to another. The routes of Roman roads are still used today in many places that were once part of the Roman Empire.

Better Trade Routes

Improvements in wheeled transportation also meant that trade grew between countries. Trade is the selling of goods for money or the exchange of one good for another. One of the most important and famous of all ancient trade roads is the Silk Road. The ancient trading route connected China to the western world. It was named the Silk Road because silk from China was taken west. Wool, gold, and silver from the west was taken east. The route was first used in around 130 BCE.

Roman roads were straight and particularly well built.

Better Boats

Not only did land transportation rapidly improve in ancient times, so did traveling by water. Early civilizations such as the ancient Egyptians and Mesopotamians used boats to transport both themselves and their goods along long stretches of water. The ancient Egyptians famously traveled up and down the Nile River using boats. They first used boats made from reeds that were woven together, and later created the boats from wood.

The ancient Egyptians were using wooden boats as early as 3400 BCE. The boats had a huge sail at their center, which captured the wind. That helped power the boats upstream on the Nile River. The inventive ancient Egyptians didn't use nails to build their boats. Instead they used short planks of wood that were shaped to hook tightly together. They were then secured with ropes.

Phoenician warships were designed for speed and power (see opposite).

BIG Breakthroughs

Ancient engineers in Egypt, China, and Mesopotamia connected their waterways by building canals. That made it possible to create a network along which people could sail boats carrying goods. That further improved trade across areas. In around 400 BCE, work on the Grand Canal in China began. This masterpiece of engineering is about 1,100 miles (1,800 km) long. The Canal connected many different river systems in China and allowed boats to travel across a huge area.

Masters of the Sea

Like the ancient Egyptians, the Phoenicians were master sailors and ship builders. They had three types of vessels. The first were warships, which were used for battle. They had a large square sail, two rows of oars, a deck, and a ram on the bow. The ram was used to slam into enemy ships. The second ship was used for transportation and trade. It was like the warship, but had a wider, bigger hull. Inside the hull a lot of goods could be contained. The ship was used to transport goods over large distances. The third type of ship was used for trade, but mainly for shorter trips. It had just one row of oars.

Stirrups to Horseshoes

Stirrups were probably first used in Asia in the second century BCE. Saddles for horse riding had been invented as early as 800 BCE. Both saddles and stirrups made horse riding much easier because they gave riders better control on a horse. By the Middle Ages, horseshoes were being used widely across Europe. The shoes meant horses could travel longer distances with fewer injuries.

The invention of the wheel allowed people to use horses and oxen to move heavier items. Horses could pull wheeled wagons for long distances.

A Smoother Ride

Wheeled vehicles such as carriages and coaches improved during the Middle Ages and beyond. Between the thirteenth and sixteenth centuries, engineers created vehicles with better suspension systems. The improved suspension meant travelers were better protected from bumps and jolts as the vehicles moved along the road. By the seventeenth century, stagecoaches were used in Europe. These coaches traveled regularly across certain routes, a little like coach buses do today.

The Industrial Revolution Begins

By the seventeenth and eighteenth centuries, invention was booming. Engineers Thomas Newcomen (1663–1729) and James Watt (1736–1819) were both making great discoveries. They figured out that the steam created when water was heated could be used to power engines. This breakthrough marked the beginning of the Industrial Revolution. Transportation was powered forward by the inventions of this period. And transportation at sea and on land were two areas that saw sweeping changes.

Steaming Ahead

Up until the seventeenth century, most vessels were sailing ships. These ships needed wind to power them. And if the weather wasn't windy, that was a problem. The invention of the steam engine led to a major engineering solution at sea: the steamship. The first steamship was invented in 1783 by a French engineer named Claude-François-Dorothée (1751–1832). The invention was very basic, but it inspired later, better vessels. American engineer Robert Fulton (1765–1815) used the same technology to create the first commercial steamboat in 1807. *The Clermont* carried people from New York City to Albany, New York, and back.

HOW IT WORKS: A STEAMSHIP

Steamships use fuel (often coal or wood) in a boiler to heat water. The water then vaporizes. That means it turns into a gas: steam. Steam can be a powerful force. The steam pushes several pistons upward. When the steam beneath the pistons is cooled, it turns back into water. That reduces the pressure beneath the pistons. The pistons then move back down. When water is heated and turned to steam again, the pistons are driven upward once more. This up-and-down movement of pistons creates the power to turn a paddlewheel or propeller. That drives the steamship forward.

Steamboats opened up transportation across waterways.

Steaming On!

Steam engines also led to a revolution in engineering on land: the steam locomotive. The locomotive is the part of a train that powers it—the engine. Today, we have steam, diesel, and even electric locomotives. However, the earliest locomotives were steam powered. The British engineer, George Stephenson (1781–1848) is known as the Father of Railways. That is because in 1825, George and his son Robert (1803–1859), built the first steam locomotive that could carry passengers on a public rail line. Five years later, they developed the first public railway line that carried people between cities. The line allowed passengers to travel between the English cities Liverpool and Manchester. It was a landmark moment that would change public transportation forever.

BIG Breakthroughs

The invention of the steamship changed the face of water transportation. Crossing the Atlantic Ocean in a sailing ship took almost twice as many days that the same voyage took in a steamship. Using steamboats meant that goods and people could be transported across oceans far more quickly. That made passenger transportation easier and more popular. It also led to quicker and easier trade.

ENGINEERING EVOLUTIONS

Discover how transportation by train has evolved in chapter 2. ►

Stephenson's *Rocket* locomotive

A Canal Across Continents

Before the eighteenth century, if people wanted to sail from Europe to Asia, they had to take a very long route. They sailed south down the coast of western Europe and Africa. Next, they traveled northeast back up the eastern coast of Africa and south of the Middle East. They then finally traveled on to southern Asia and the Far East. A solution was needed to make this shipping route easier and quicker: the Suez Canal. Building work on the Suez Canal began in 1859 and was completed in 1869. The canal connects the Mediterranean Sea to the Red Sea. It is 120 miles (193 km) long. By using the canal, the trip from Europe to Asia was reduced by thousands of miles.

The Suez Canal is one of the world's busiest waterways.

Work began on the Panama Canal in 1881 and was completed by 1914. It was an amazing feat of engineering.

Across the Americas

The Suez Canal solved the issue of water transportation between Europe and Asia. However, getting between the western and eastern sides of the Americas was still a major problem. For a ship to sail from New York to San Francisco, they had to sail south down the Atlantic Ocean, all the way around the tip of South America. Next, they had to make their way back up the west coast of South America, Central America, and the western United States. It was a long way. It could also be deadly. An easier route was needed. And so, the Panama Canal was built across Panama, the narrowest part of Central America.

Engineering the Canal

Designing the Panama Canal took a lot of engineering thought. Panama has a large lake that is higher than the Atlantic and Pacific Oceans. Panama is also mountainous. Engineers realized that ships would need to be raised and lowered to make the distance. Gatun Lake is 85 feet (26 m) above sea level, and the canal had to be raised to reach that level. That is called gaining elevation. To make the elevation possible, three locks were built to lift the ships to the height of Gatun Lake. Three more locks lower the ships. In addition, a deep 8-mile (13 km) channel had to be cut through the mountains.

HOW IT WORKS:
A LOCK SYSTEM

A lock is a little like an elevator for vessels. For a ship to gain elevation in a lock system, the following steps are needed:

1. The lock is drained of water through underground channels. That lowers the water level.
2. The lower gate is opened, allowing the ship to enter the lock.
3. The gates are closed once the ship is in the lock. The drainage system is closed to stop any more water from draining out.
4. A top sluice is opened, allowing water to enter the lock from the higher elevation.
5. As the water level rises, the ship is lifted.
6. When the ship reaches the correct elevation, the top gate is opened. The ship then leaves the lock.

For a ship to be lowered, the steps are reversed.

Hitting the Road by Bicycle

In the nineteenth century, great leaps forward took place in land transportation too. The first bicycle-like machine was invented by a German named Karl von Drais (1785–1851) in 1817. It had two wheels but no pedals, so users pushed it forward with their feet. Next came the "boneshaker." This early bicycle was created in the 1860s. It had pedals and was made of wood and metal. However, it made for a very bumpy ride, which is how it got its name.

The Grandfather of Modern Bikes

High-wheel bicycles were next on the road. They were invented between the 1870s and 1880s. They had a very big front wheel and a small back wheel. Pedals were connected to the front wheel only and turned it. The big front wheel helped the bikes travel faster. The wheel's size meant it covered more distance with each turn. However, riders could easily fall off the tall bikes. In 1885, a much safer bike was invented by English engineer John Kemp Starley (1854–1901). It had two equally sized wheels, which made it much safer to ride. It also had a chain drive that connected the pedals to the rear wheel too. It is known as the safety bike and is the grandfather of all modern bikes.

Early bikes were not easy to ride!

Hitting the Road by Car

The first car for everyday use was built in 1885 by German engineer Karl Benz (1844–1929). This new vehicle was powered by an internal-combustion engine. In 1888, Benz's company Benz & Co started selling the car. However, it was too expensive for most people to afford. Then, in 1903, Henry Ford (1863–1947) created the Ford Motor Company. His Ford Model T car went on sale in 1908. It changed transportation on the roads forever.

This Ford car was built in 1915.

ENGINEERING SOLUTIONS

Before the Ford Motor Company, cars were expensive to buy. That is because they took a long time to build. Cars were built in one position, with several workers working on the vehicle at the same time. Ford then introduced the assembly line in 1913. The assembly line was a system in which the parts needed for a car were made before the car was built. The car was then assembled, or put together, using those parts. One worker would add one part, and the car would then move down the line. Another worker would add another part, and the car would move along the line again. This process then continued, one section at a time, until the car was complete.

The assembly line was a much quicker way to put a car together than the traditional way. Producing cars using this new, smart method increased the number of vehicles that could be made. It also reduced the costs of making them. As a result, Ford was able to sell his cars more cheaply, and they became more affordable for most people.

Flying High

People have always been fascinated by flight, and great minds have tried to figure out how to get into the air for centuries. Italian inventor and artist Leonardo da Vinci (1452–1519) famously spent hours trying to design machines that could fly. He made more than 200 sketches of different flying machines! However, flight didn't really get started until a few hundred years later. In 1783, the Montgolfier brothers in France launched the first manned hot-air balloon. That was the first-ever flight for humans. That same year, the first manned hydrogen balloon flight also took place in France.

People were amazed by the first hot-air balloons!

Gliding Along

In the late 1800s, a German engineer named Otto Lilienthal (1848–1896) worked on the idea of using gliders for flight. Lilienthal was the first person to make successful glider flights. He soon became known as the "flying man." Gliders do not have engines. Instead, they glide through the air using the natural lift of air currents.

The First Powered Air Flight

Building on the work of earlier engineers, the brothers Orville (1871–1948) and Wilbur Wright (1867–1912) experimented further with gliders. They wanted to know how to add power to a glider. This was key to being able to launch an airplane from flat ground. That is because gliders needed a way to lift into the air before they could ride on its currents. Eventually, the brothers successfully made the first powered airplane flight. It took place in 1903 near Kitty Hawk, North Carolina. It was a landmark moment.

The Wright brothers' first powered airplane

HOW IT WORKS:
FLIGHT CONTROL

Part of the challenge of flight was not just aircraft weight, but also control. Airplanes have three angles of rotation, or turning, around their center of mass. They are the roll, the pitch, and the yaw. To understand how this works, picture an imaginary pole that runs through an airplane from nose to tail:

The roll: Picture the plane rotating on that imaginary pole, with one wing up and the opposite wing down. Without any stabilization, the plane could spin wing-over-wing on this imaginary pole.

The pitch: Now picture that same imaginary pole being wiggled up and down. The plane would rock with the nose up and tail down, or the tail up and nose down. Without any stabilization, the plane could do tail-over-nose cartwheels.

The yaw: Picture the imaginary pole removed. Then imagine it instead stuck vertically through the plane's center of mass (roughly in the center of the plane, lengthwise). Without stabilization, the plane could spin around to the left or right. It would move and change direction just like a car turns left or right.

Fixing Flight

The Wright brothers addressed the issue of flight control by developing a three-axis control system. This allowed the pilot to control the plane's pitch, yaw, and roll. The pilot could constantly adjust the plane's behavior in the air. They would adjust it depending on the flight, changes in height, weather conditions, and direction. Their three-axis control system is still used in airplanes today.

ENGINEERING EVOLUTIONS

Discover how air travel has evolved from the time of the Wright brothers to today in chapter 3.

Jetting Around the World

In the early 1920s, the first commercial air travel for passengers began. The Pan American World Airways (Pan Am) was created in 1927 and soon became an international air travel company. From the 1930s onward, commercial aircraft design got better and better. Then in the 1950s, things really took off. The first commercial jet service was offered in 1952 by British Overseas Airways Corporation (BOAC). It traveled from London, England, to Johannesburg, South Africa. In 1958, the Boeing 707 was introduced. It was the first commercial jet airliner used for long-haul flights. It changed long-distance air travel forever, by making it quicker and more affordable. The age of air travel and overseas vacations really began to take off.

BIG Breakthroughs

In 1976, the first supersonic aircraft to be used for commercial flights came about: the Concorde airplane. Supersonic air travel is when a plane flies faster than the speed of sound. Sound travels at about 768 miles per hour (1,236 kph)—also known as Mach 1. Anything traveling faster than Mach 1 has broken the sound barrier and is a supersonic flight. The Concorde reached speeds of up to 1,354 miles per hour (2,180 kph). That was more than twice the speed of sound. Concorde airplanes could fly from New York City to London in 2 hours and 52 minutes. A regular passenger jet generally takes close to 7 hours to travel the same route. Concorde was a game changer. But flights were stopped in 2003, because of concerns about cost, safety factors, and the effect on the environment. The sonic boom created by the planes was part of the reason for those environmental concerns.

Concorde in flight

ENGINEERING EVOLUTIONS

Discover how improved supersonic air travel could make a comeback in chapter 3.

Supersonic aircraft move so quickly that they disturb air molecules as they travel.

A Sonic Boom

When a plane breaks the sound barrier, it creates a sonic boom. It sounds like a loud explosion. This is because when the plane moves through the air, it creates pressure waves. They are a little like the ripples that you can see in a lake when you toss a stone into it. The same thing happens with pressure waves created when a plane flies at speeds below Mach 1. However, when a plane flies at or above the speed of sound, those pressure waves build up and squash together. They form one big wave known as a shockwave. This wave moves at the speed of sound, but since the aircraft is traveling faster, it effectively outruns the sound waves it produces. The result is a sudden pressure shift that creates a sonic boom, heard as a loud cracking noise.

Twenty-First Century Evolutions

Huge leaps in engineering have been made in the twentieth century. They are the result of great engineering. Today's engineers are building on that engineering knowledge. They are also turning to ancient engineering to inspire modern transportation ideas. However, they have a new and important challenge: making transportation sustainable. That means engineers are having to create even more inventive technology. Engineering in transportation is evolving to become greener and more efficient than ever.

CHAPTER 2

A LAND EVOLUTION

Traveling by automobile is costly–both financially and environmentally.

Moving across land has been revolutionized in modern times by amazing engineering developments. Bicycles, automobiles, and trains have all been upgraded. They are faster, more efficient, and more environmentally friendly. And people have found inventive ways to move vehicles below the ground as well as above it.

The Cost of Driving

Automobiles are by far the most popular way to get around in the United States and throughout the world. Two major issues in automobile travel are the cost of gasoline and the environmental impact of gas-powered vehicles. Gas prices vary a lot, for example, depending on location and because of supply and demand. According to the US Department of Energy (DoE), the average miles per gallon for a car in 2024 was 24.4. Light trucks and vans averaged 17.8 miles per gallon. That means in an area with high gasoline prices, it could cost as much as $28 to drive a car 100 miles (160 km). It would cost $39 to drive a light truck that same distance.

Cars and the Environment

The US Environmental Protection Agency (EPA) says that the average car emits about 4.5 tons (4.6 mt) of carbon dioxide each year. Carbon dioxide is a harmful greenhouse gas. This is a gas that when pumped into the air, collects in Earth's atmosphere. There, along with other harmful gases, it forms a "blanket" that surrounds the planet, causing it to warm up. That is called global warming. To try to reduce global warming, engineers are working hard to lower the amount of gasoline vehicles use. They are also working to remove gasoline as a fuel altogether. These important steps will pave the way to cleaner transportation.

New Cars on the Roads

Hybrid and electric cars are part of the solution to gasoline-powered vehicles. Hybrid cars are sometimes powered by electricity and sometimes powered by gas. That depends on how much electrical power is available to the engine at any given time. In contrast, all-electric cars are completely powered by electricity. They have a battery that is charged at a charging point. The battery then provides electricity to power an electric motor, which drives the wheels. Both hybrid and electric cars produce fewer greenhouse gas emissions when compared with a traditional gas-powered engine.

HOW IT WORKS:
A HYBRID ENGINE

There are two types of hybrid engine: a standard hybrid and a plug-in hybrid.

Standard hybrid: This system has both a gas-powered engine and an electric motor. When the driver takes their foot off the gas or uses the brakes, the energy created is turned into electricity. The electricity is stored in a battery pack, so it can be later used to power the car. This is called a regenerative braking system. When possible, the car switches from using power from the gas engine to electricity from the electric motor.

Plug-in hybrid: This engine is like a standard hybrid engine, but it also has an electric charge port. The driver can recharge the car through the port. The energy from recharging is stored in the battery pack. Recharging means more energy can be stored than through regenerative braking alone. That means the car can be driven farther on electric power.

Some regenerative braking systems have now become so efficient that vehicles can recapture more than 70 percent of their breaking energy. That means the cars can be driven farther without needing to recharge.

A car's predictive energy optimization system provides the vehicle with more energy when moving uphill.

New Ways of Driving

Another breakthrough in car technology is building cars that can adapt how they make and use energy depending on the conditions they drive in. Today, many green cars have inbuilt eco-driving modes. These are systems that automatically adjust the way the car drives to make it more energy efficient. For example, they reduce the power the car uses at times when it is moving across easy, flat terrain. Then the power output of the car is increased when needed. For example, that might be when moving across uphill terrain or other challenging surfaces.

Cars are also designed with systems that use different data to predict when they will need the most energy. That prediction is based on the route the car will take and its terrain. It also factors in the amount of expected traffic on the route. The information is then used to control the power output of the car. This intelligent automobile system is known as predictive energy optimization.

HOW IT WORKS:

PREDICTIVE ENERGY OPTIMIZATION

Real-time information from different sources is collected. It is then used to make smart predictions about the energy a car will use on a given route. The car's navigation system provides information about the route. That includes detail about distance, speed limits, and other factors. Real-time traffic updates help the system figure out where the car may need to slow down or stop. Weather conditions are also factored in. The typical driving behavior of the driver is also used.

Once all the data is in place, the system uses an algorithm to figure out the most energy-efficient way to deal with each section of the route. For example, it will adjust power output to save energy on hilly routes. In a fully electric car, more battery power is used to travel uphill. Using more regenerative braking downhill recaptures energy. It is then built back into the car's energy system. The predictive system might reduce power output in parts of the route where stop-and-go traffic is likely. It will use regenerative braking in these situations too.

In hybrid cars, the system will use similar methods, but will also decide when to use the electric motor and the internal-combustion engine. For example, it may use the electric motor in city traffic then switch to the internal-combustion engine when driving on highways. That dual use makes for the most energy-efficient type of driving.

Smart Energy Exchanges

Cars may become so energy efficient that they can send energy back to the grid rather than using it! That is known as vehicle-to-grid (V2G) technology. It is currently being developed by car manufacturers such as Nissan and Ford. One of the vehicles from Ford, the Ford F-150 Lightning, can be charged at a person's home. It can then provide energy to that home during emergencies, such as power outages: a win-win for owners.

The Nissan Leaf has V2G technology.

Help from Hydrogen

Hydrogen fuel cell electric vehicles (FCEVs) are another breakthrough technology in the car industry. These vehicles use hydrogen as a source of fuel rather than relying on rechargeable batteries. FCEVs are made up of a tank that stores hydrogen gas. They also have a fuel cell stack, which is made up of many fuel cells. The cars have an electric motor and a battery, which stores any extra energy made by the car.

Refueling with Hydrogen

To refuel a FCEV, the driver connects a pump nozzle to an inlet on the vehicle. The hydrogen is then pumped into the car's tank. This works in the same way that a pump is used to put gasoline from a tank into a car. However, rather than gasoline, hydrogen is pumped into the car from a tank using special equipment.

HOW IT WORKS: AN FCEV

Each fuel cell creates electricity when a reaction between hydrogen and oxygen takes place. Hydrogen gas from the car's fuel tank is fed into the cell. There it chemically reacts with oxygen from the air, releasing energy in the process. That then creates an electric current that powers the car's electric motor. The only byproduct of the process is water vapor, which leaves the car through the exhaust. The car is therefore completely free of harmful emissions.

A hydrogen fuel cell battery

This vehicle is being refueled with hydrogen.

The Good and the Bad

Hydrogen-powered vehicles have many advantages over both gasoline-powered cars and electric cars. Unlike gasoline-powered cars, they produce no emissions, so are fully environmentally friendly. Electric cars may take a while to recharge and may need to be recharged often. Hydrogen-powered cars take just a few minutes to refuel, like a gasoline-powered car. That makes them more convenient for drivers who want to cover longer distances while quickly refueling. Hydrogen cars can also cover distances similar to a gasoline car, roughly 300 to 400 miles (482 to 643 km) per tank. That makes them better suited to long-distance travel.

The drawbacks of the cars are mainly their cost and availability. Hydrogen refueling stations are expensive to build and maintain. It is also expensive to make both a fuel cell and hydrogen. For those reasons, the cars are currently too expensive for most people to buy.

Looking to the Future

Car companies such as Toyota and Hyundai are improving the design of their fuel cell stacks. That will reduce the cost of buying a FCEV. It will make the driving range of the vehicles far longer too. The technology is improving at such a rate that more hydrogen refueling stations are being created in areas such as California, Japan, and parts of Europe. Once the technology of the vehicles reaches a point at which it can be rolled out widely, more and more hydrogen refueling stations will appear elsewhere. That will make long-range, zero-emission driving a reality.

Cars That Drive Themselves

Decades ago, the idea of an autonomous, or self-driving, car seemed the stuff of science-fiction movies. Yet self-driving cars are now here. However, it is only on certain test areas that *fully* autonomous cars are currently allowed. They are not yet available to buy. That is because the vehicles are still being tested for safety. However, there are cars available to the public that offer a certain amount of autonomous driving. The vehicles are organized into levels of autonomy. Only certain levels are available to most people.

Autonomous driving vehicles are organized into levels.

Level	Name	Description
1	Driver assistance	Some assistance with steering, acceleration, or deceleration depending on the surroundings, such as if the car in front is too close.
2	Partial automation	System activates changes to steering or acceleration while the driver is there if necessary. Driver is still in charge of the vehicle.
3	Conditional automation	Automated systems perform all aspects of driving, with driver intervening if necessary.
4	High automation	Automated systems perform all aspects of driving, even if driver does not intervene. May not operate in all locations and conditions, such as bad weather.
5	Full automation	Automated systems perform all aspects of driving in all locations and conditions. Human driver not required.

Leading the Way

Car manufacturer Tesla has led the way in autonomous vehicles. The company has created cars that provide level 2 autonomy. They can be driven hands-free on highways, with the driver supervising. General Motors and Ford have created level 2 cars that allow for hands-free driving on certain mapped highways in North America. Again, the driver must be alert and ready to take control in all instances. In Europe, Mercedes Benz has created a level 3 system that allows autonomous driving on highways up to 60 miles per hour (95 kph), but again only in specific areas and driving conditions.

HOW IT WORKS:
A SELF-DRIVING CAR

Autonomous vehicles use a wide range of sensors to gather data about their location and the environment around them:

- LiDAR sends millions of laser pulses to build a complex model of the vehicle's surroundings.
- Radar uses electromagnetic waves to identify objects such as other vehicles.
- Cameras gather visual data, such as traffic lights, construction signs, and street markings.
- Other sensors fix the car's position and pick up sounds such as police sirens.
- Software processes all this data to build a complete picture of the environment and so plan how the vehicle should respond. It uses machine learning to predict how vehicles and people will move.

Self-driving cars use inbuilt sensor systems to pick up the location of objects around them.

Waymo taxis take people around San Francisco—with no driver required.

Driverless Taxis

Some companies have also created autonomous taxis to transport people around cities. In the United States the companies Waymo and Cruise offer robotaxi services in Phoenix and San Francisco. Some of the first taxis were launched in San Francisco. The city is tricky to navigate, with a lot of steep and narrow streets and heavy traffic. The idea is that the artificial intelligence (AI) systems controlling the cars will learn faster in an environment with more dangers. That will lead to quicker and more far-reaching improvements in the technology.

Moving Many People

Transporting many people at the same time is known as mass transit. There have been some exciting innovations in this area of transportation too. New bus technology is one of them. Many of the world's cities are moving from diesel or gasoline-powered buses to electric vehicles. They are doing so to cut harmful emissions, noise, and improve the quality of air in those cities. Los Angeles, London, and Shenzhen in China have all brought in electric buses to transport the people around the cities in a more environmentally friendly way.

Trolley and Tram Takeover

Electric trolleys and trams are also providing a great alternative to gas-guzzling vehicles in some cities. Monterey, California, has introduced all-electric trolleys to its bus fleet. These trolleys are free to ride and take people to some of the more congested areas of town. The trolleys charge at charging stations at trolley stops. On a larger scale, the city of Adelaide, Australia, has a fleet of solar-powered buses that are free to ride. The bus stations in the city have solar panels to create electricity and batteries to store the power. The buses then recharge at the stations. The buses also have a regenerative braking system.

One of Adelaide's solar-powered electric buses

Hydrogen's Helping Hand

Just as hydrogen fuel cells are being used in car technology, they are in buses too. Germany is a world leader in creating hydrogen fuel cell buses. The UK too has introduced the vehicles in some cities, including London. Also on the roads are self-driving buses. France has worked driverless shuttles into some of its city centers. They carry people short distances across the city. There are plans too to run the buses in more rural areas. Singapore, in Asia, and Las Vegas are two more areas in which autonomous buses are being tested with a view to wider roll-out.

Loop systems could make traveling around cities faster and easier.

ENGINEERING SOLUTIONS

Infrastructure is a big issue in transportation. Many busy roads are already clogged with travelers and cannot absorb a lot more. Elon Musk's Boring Company aims to provide a solution to this issue. It has plans to create tunnels to transport people underground between busy areas, reducing congestion on the roads. The company calls its networks of tunnels Loops. One of the first operating Loop system is planned for Las Vegas. Passengers will be transported between busy areas by electric vehicle.

Other companies are experimenting with loop systems also. They include Virgin, which developed the Virgin Hyperloop. This concept is based on creating pods in which people would travel. The pods would pass through tubes that are designed to reduce air resistance. That would allow the pods to travel at speeds of up to 760 miles per hour (1,220 kph). The pods would contain up to 28 passengers and run along routes to connect cities such as Los Angeles and San Francisco. The project is currently on hold, however, while the company focuses on other plans.

Superfast Trains

High-speed trains have transformed modern-day travel by rail. These trains can reach incredibly fast speeds of between 155 miles per hour (250 kph) and 375 miles per hour (603 kph). The trains are designed to be as aerodynamic as possible, with sleek, smooth bodies. They have advanced signaling systems. That means many trains can run safely at the same time on the same network.

The trains run on specially built tracks that can handle the vehicles' high speeds. The tracks also have only gentle curves. That allows the trains to run safely at very high speeds. Very curvy lines would derail the trains, or make them come off their tracks. The trains are usually powered by electricity. This makes them efficient and more environmentally friendly than diesel-powered trains.

Trains That Float

Some trains, such as Maglev trains, do not use wheels and traditional tracks. Instead, they "float" above a magnetic track. Magnetism pushes the train along the track, so that it follows its route. However, because the train does not come into contact with the track, no friction is created. Friction is a force that slows down objects when they touch a surface while traveling across it. The lack of friction means that Maglev trains can travel at very high speeds. No contact with the track also means the trains are very quiet.

Maglev trains move at high speed both smoothly and quietly.

HOW IT WORKS:
A MAGLEV TRAIN

Maglev is short for magnetic levitation. The trains are suspended just above the tracks by using magnet technology known as electromagnetic propulsion. This is the same force you feel when you hold two magnets near each other and the opposite poles repel, or push each other away. The force created when the magnets repel each other is partly what allows the trains to be suspended over the track.

An Emissions Win

Maglev trains are environmentally friendly. Since they are powered by electricity, they are zero-emissions vehicles. Building the trains and the tracks they run on does cause some environmental harm, however. But generally the trains are an efficient and environmentally friendly way to travel.

Several cities around the world run Maglev trains. They include Shanghai in China, Hamburg in Germany, and Seoul in South Korea. The trains have provided a solution to traffic congestion and air pollution in these cities, where many people live. A lot of people use the Maglev trains to travel to and from work. They also use them to get around the cities for other means. That has reduced people's need for other less environmentally friendly forms of transportation, such as cars.

The Shinkansen is also known as the "bullet train." It is one of the world's most famous high-speed trains. The bullet train runs in Japan and can reach speeds of up to 200 miles per hour (320 kph).

People use the metro in Dubai to make their way across the city.

Driverless Trains Under the Ground

Just as self-driving cars exist on our roads, so too do self-driving trains in our cities—but under the ground. They run smoothly and efficiently on metro networks in many of the world's greatest cities. In Paris, France, the city's metro Line 14 runs a fully automated metro line. Two more of its lines, Line 1 and Line 4, are also automated. The Singapore metro operates several autonomous train lines. So too does the Dubai metro, in the United Arab Emirates (UAE). In Vancouver, Canada, the SkyTrain also runs without drivers. It stretches for more than 49 miles (80 km) and has many lines along which driverless trains run. There are now many plans for fully automated metro lines worldwide.

Above the Ground for Goods

Above the ground too driverless trains are in operation. Some carry goods across long distances. For example, Rio Tinto is a company that is testing driverless freight trains in remote parts of Australia. In areas where few towns and cities are found, it is easy to create long stretches of railroad that can carry driverless trains to test how safe they will be.

The AutoHaul project run by Rio Tinto is a fully autonomous freight train system in Western Australia. The trains that run on the tracks there transport iron ore. They carry it from mines inland to ports on the coast, with no driver on board. The trains are controlled remotely by both operators and automated control systems.

Above the Ground for People

There are also some autonomous passenger trains currently running above ground, but they are still quite rare. However, like the freight train transportation projects in testing in Australia, similar projects for passenger trains are being run in several countries. In France, a company is working on a hydrogen-powered train that is partly autonomous. The project is named Coradia iLint. It has driver-assisted systems currently in place, which in the future could become fully automated. In Germany researchers are experimenting with using AI to manage train movement, signaling, and emergency handling.

This hydrogen-powered train operates in Germany. In the future, trains such as this may be fully automated.

ENGINEERING SOLUTIONS

A lot of people are concerned about driverless trains and how safe they are, just as there are concerns about self-driving cars. For that reason, engineers have built key features into many autonomous trains. These include:

Automatic train control: Inbuilt systems automatically manage and control the train's speed and braking. They monitor track conditions and use real-time information to control the train, making sure it operates safely.

Communication control: Technology that allows real-time communication between trains and control centers keeps traffic flowing smoothly and prevents collisions.

Sensors: Automatic trains have state-of-the-art sensors. That allows them to detect objects nearby or on the track. It also helps them monitor weather and detect other trains.

Remote monitoring and control: Many systems allow remote operators to control the trains when needed. For example, they can take control of the vehicle in an emergency.

Earth-Friendly Transportations

Electronic bicycles, or e-bikes, are one of the most environmentally friendly forms of modern transportation. Some studies have shown that e-bikes are up to 35 times more efficient to run than electric cars. In fact, most of the emissions created by e-bikes come from making them rather than using them.

Helping the Rider

E-bikes have an electric motor. It provides extra power to assist the rider with their pedaling. The bike's motor helps drive the wheels around. The motor is powered by a rechargeable battery. A controller acts like the "brain" of the bike. It controls the flow of power from the battery to the motor. The rider can control how much pedal assistance is given by using an assist level control, which ranges from 1 to 5. Level 1 is the lowest amount of assistance. Level 5 provides the most assistance.

Faster and More Comfortable

E-bike design has improved a lot in recent years. Bikes have become more aerodynamic. They pass through air with as little resistance as possible. Air resistance is called drag, and it slows down a vehicle. Being aerodynamic means e-bikes travel quickly, and many bikes have improved suspension systems. Some even have electronically controlled suspension systems. These adjust in real time, depending on the terrain the rider is traveling across. That makes for a more comfortable ride. The bikes also have automatic gear-shifting technology. That means the bikes immediately adjust gears based on the speed at which they are traveling and the terrain they are covering. That makes for easier and more efficient cycling.

A lot of modern e-bikes have tubeless tires and puncture-resistant technology. That means getting a puncture is far less likely, which makes the bikes more suitable for city commuting. They can also handle more serious off-road biking in rural areas too.

Many bikes have inbuilt LED lights. Some even have turn signals. Both make riding at night and in towns and cities a lot easier and safer.

BIG Breakthroughs

Other technological advances in the bikes include global positioning system (GPS) and tracking systems. Many e-bikes have inbuilt GPS tracking systems that help the rider find their way. They also help track the bike if it is stolen. Riders can connect their bikes to smartphone apps to plan routes and also adjust them while on the bike. Some smart bikes now use AI to check the bikes for maintenance. AI can check to see if the brakes, chains, tires, and other parts of the bike are road-worthy. It alerts the rider if repairs are needed.

Bigger and Better

E-bikes are now often made using materials such as carbon fiber, which are strong and lightweight. Titanium alloys are sometimes used too in the vehicles. That makes them less likely to rust so that they last longer. E-cargo bikes are bikes that are designed to carry heavy loads or many passengers at once. These bikes are great for delivering packages in towns and cities, including food deliveries. They are also ideal for family transportation, such as getting children to and from school. The bikes have bigger and stronger frames that can handle the extra weight of more passengers. They are built with more powerful motors and larger batteries too.

CHAPTER 3

AN AIR EVOLUTION

Engineers are coming up with ways to limit the environmental damage caused by airplanes.

Since the early propeller-powered airplanes of the early twentieth century and the jet plane age of the 1950s and 1970s, air travel has come on in leaps and bounds. Jet plane travel has allowed people to travel all over the world. However, there are many environmental concerns about jet planes. The planes are powered by internal-combustion engines. Jet fuel and air are forced into combustion chambers in the engine. There they ignite, or catch fire. The exhaust gases produced by the ignition of the fuel and air are released from the back of the engine. That propels the plane forward, but also releases greenhouse gases into the environment. With rising concerns about global warming and climate change, the race is on for engineers to find more sustainable forms of air travel.

Turning to Hybrid

Just as hybrid cars have hit the roads, hybrid vehicles are taking to the air. Hybrid airplanes work in a similar way to hybrid cars, by providing power from both gasoline and electricity. They do so with a hybrid-electric turbofan jet engine. Using electricity reduces the amount of fossil fuel burned for energy. That means fewer greenhouse gas emissions, which is good for the planet.

HOW IT WORKS:

A HYBRID-ELECTRIC TURBOFAN JET ENGINE

A turbofan engine works by drawing in air through a fan. The air flows into the center of the engine. There it is combined with fuel. The combined air and fuel is ignited. That creates a powerful chemical reaction, which releases a lot of energy in the form of hot expanding gases. This is combustion. The gases then rush through the turbine to another fan, causing it to spin. When the gases leave the engine that creates thrust.

In a hybrid-electric engine, the electric system works alongside the gas turbine system. An electric motor helps create thrust or takes over the creation of it altogether. The electric motor may be used at times when a lot of thrust is needed, such as takeoff. That reduces the amount of fuel needed for the flight. That in turn reduces emissions and noise levels as the electric system is quieter than conventional combustion.

Smaller Could Be Better

The National Aeronautics and Space Administration (NASA) is trying to make the hybrid airplane model even more Earth-friendly. It is developing a small core for hybrid-electric turbofan jet engines. Since the core of a traditional jet engine is where the combustion takes place, if it is smaller less fuel may be needed. That will lead to lower carbon emissions. The Hybrid Thermally Efficient Core (HyTEC) may be able to reduce fuel burn by about 10 percent.

Scientists are working on improvements to the hybrid-electric turbofan jet engine.

Turboprop aircraft could make air transportation to many parts of the world both easier and less damaging to the environment.

Earth-Friendly Flying

Another engineering solution to the issue of using fossil fuels for flight are turboprop planes. These aircraft use gas power to make the propellers turn. That then generates the thrust needed to push the plane forward. The turboprop engine has a section called an intake, which draws in air. The air is then compressed in the engine and is then added to fuel in the combustion chamber. Fuel and air combusts, and the resulting expanding hot gases pass through a turbine, making it spin, before escaping as exhaust. This turbine is connected to a drive shaft that powers the propeller.

That sounds typical of a jet plane, so how are these planes better for the environment? Well, turboprops need less fuel than jet engines. Better fuel efficiency means lower fares can be passed on to the customer. That also makes the turboprops cheaper to use. That is good news for carrier companies and travelers. Also turboprops are generally smaller than private jets. That means they can handle the shorter runways that bigger planes cannot use. That means the turboprops can use many of the smaller airports around the world that have short runways that standard planes cannot use.

Going Supersonic

As well as wanting cheaper travel, people want to get where they are going as quickly as possible. The hunt is constantly on for faster air travel, but with less impact to the environment. In general, passenger jets fly more slowly than the speed of sound. When fully in the air after takeoff, passenger jets fly most of their route at about 500 miles per hour (805 kph). Supersonic air travel beats that hands down, with supersonic planes traveling far faster than the speed of sound

In the past, supersonic travel was halted due to concerns about its cost. The jets are very expensive to build and run. That made flying on a supersonic jet very expensive. They also use a lot of fuel and are very noisy. That led to real concerns about the impact on the environment. But some engineers think that supersonic could make a comeback if the issues that surround it could be fixed with some smart engineering.

ENGINEERING SOLUTIONS

NASA and other aviation companies are looking at ways to improve the existing technology and make travel by supersonic jet a reality again. NASA has a test jet that could fly up to Mach 4. It could make the trip from New York City to London in just 90 minutes! To avoid noise problems, engineers are working on the plane's body shape. They are designing it to spread out the shockwaves that supersonic planes create. That way, the sonic boom won't be an issue.

Many military aircraft fly at supersonic speeds. With improvements in engineering, passenger aircraft could once more fly at superfast speeds.

Amazon's drone delivery system could become the way goods are delivered to our homes and businesses in the future.

Delivered by Drones

Although drone technology cannot help with transporting passengers, it is a great tool for moving goods around by air. Drones are small, unmanned flying vehicles that can carry goods over short distances. Several companies have been testing autonomous drones for cargo delivery. Amazon is one of them. The company's Prime Air division is building drones that can deliver packages weighing up to 5 pounds (2.3 kg). They will be able to do so over a 15-mile (24 km) radius. When it comes to traveling farther, the airline company Boeing is working on drones that could transport goods over long distances. The vehicles could be used to carry goods to remote or difficult-to-reach places.

BIG Breakthroughs

Some autonomous drones are piloted by AI systems. In 2023, a small autonomous drone controlled by AI was pitched against the best human drone operators. They went head-to-head in a race round a complex course. They had to dodge obstacles at speeds of around 100 miles per hour (160 kph). The AI drones won hands-down. They showed that AI could navigate a difficult course and make quick decisions. That could make AI-controlled drones especially useful when navigating difficult terrain or built-up places such as cities.

Self-Driving Airplanes

Just as self-driving trains are being tested for use on land, so too are self-driving aircraft. Currently, the testing of vehicles is mainly for cargo transportation. Engineers are working on autonomous hybrid aircraft that combine airplane and drone technology. These aircraft can carry goods that are heavier than those normally transported by drone. They can also carry them over longer distances. Experts also predict that fully autonomous passenger aircraft may not be far away.

Artificial Air Travel

Planning routes, monitoring weather, and tracking other air vehicles is time-consuming. Yet, it is an important part of air travel. Currently, people carry out these tasks. However, AI technology is advancing to a point at which it could take over. That would help companies better plan flights and analyze data to make cost savings. For example, Alaska Airlines has started using AI tools to plan flights. It was able to schedule flights to avoid bad weather or busy landing slots. The system saved about 480,000 gallons (1,816,000 l) of fuel in 6 months and cut flight times.

In the future, as self-driving airplane technology becomes a reality for passenger flights, AI could be very effective. It would make things easier for passengers, such as using facial recognition to check identities. That could mean the current passport checks used in air travel are no longer needed, which would speed up boarding.

Facial recognition systems could remove the need for time-consuming checks in airports in the future.

Other Ways to Travel by Air

Helicopters are not used by most people for regular transportation. That is mainly because they do not hold many people. Another issue with helicopters is that they fly at lower altitudes than airplanes, which means weather is more of a factor. However, new innovations may solve the issue of helicopters and other smaller aircraft flying at lower altitudes. One of them is the Leonardo AW609. This vehicle looks like a small plane. It can hold up to 9 passengers. That is similar to a small private jet. It can fly more than twice the speed of a regular helicopter and has a pressurized cabin that allows it to fly at around 25,000 feet (7,620 m). This altitude is much higher than that a standard helicopter flies at. That allows the Leonardo AW609 to climb above areas of difficult weather, such as heavy rain.

The Leonardo AW609

A Vertical Solution

One exciting innovation on the engineering horizon is the electric vertical takeoff and landing (eVTOL). This is an aircraft that uses electric propulsion systems to take off, hover, and land vertically. Vertical takeoff and landing does not require a runway. This type of air transportation could be a gamechanger in congested cities, providing quick and easy air travel.

HOW IT WORKS: AN EVTOL

All eVTOLs are powered by electric motors. The motors drive propellers or rotors. The electricity comes from onboard batteries or sometimes from hydrogen fuel cells. During takeoff, the vehicles use many rotors, moving vertically like a helicopter. Once high enough, the vehicles move forward. They land like a helicopter too, moving vertically toward the ground.

Big Benefits

eVTOL transportation has many benefits, including not needing a runway. The vehicles are much quieter than traditional aircraft because they use electric motors. They produce zero emissions, which makes them environmentally friendly. They use little space because they need no runway. That means they can be used in built-up urban areas where there is not enough room for a runway. They can also be used in remote, rural locations that do not have runways.

Testing the Technology

Just a few areas of the world currently have eVTOLs. Most are used for demonstration and test flights. That is because the technology is new and constantly being improved. However, the vehicles have been used on sightseeing flights in China and Dubai. They are also being trialed for use in emergency services, such as transporting medical supplies to where they are needed. In the United States, trial flights are planned for Los Angeles. Other short-distance routes in remaining parts of California are also in the works.

eVTOL vehicles are currently only in the planning stage, but if the engineering works, they could become a real part of our transportation future.

CHAPTER 4

A WATER EVOLUTION

Throughout the twentieth century, most boats and ships were powered by fossil fuels. That energy use has damaged the planet. But just as engineers have cleaned up transportation on land and in the air, they are doing the same on water. They are finding ways to make ships, ferries, and boats more efficient and environmentally friendly. That includes using alternative forms of power. Electric, hybrid, solar, and wind power are all on the menu. Better design of vessels is also making a difference. And AI technology is helping engineers explore self-driving vehicles or partly autonomous vehicles.

Turning to Electric and Hybrid

Like land and air vehicles, engineering solutions for vehicles on water are relying more and more on electric or hybrid models. Electric-powered ferries are being used by many countries. These vessels are powered by batteries or fuel cells. The Ellen Ferry in Denmark is a good example of a fully electric ferry. It can carry up to 200 passengers and 30 cars 22 nautical miles (40 km) between the islands of Ærø and Als. It recharges via a charging arm on the harbor ramp and is the largest electric ferry in the world. It has set a record of traveling 50 nautical miles (92 km) on one charge! Another European country has also introduced electric ferries. Norway's Ampere ferry uses batteries to reduce carbon emissions.

All-Electric in North America

In California, the Golden Gate Ferry is also introducing electric ferries. It has plans to replace older diesel-powered ferries with electric-powered vehicles. Washington State Ferries too is moving into electric ferries. The organization already has a hybrid-electric ferry, which runs a service from Seattle to Bainbridge Island. It plans to operate only hybrid-electric ferries by 2040. Similar plans for electric ferries are also underway in New York City.

In Canada, British Columbia Ferries has launched its first electric ferry service. The Island Class ferries run on battery-electric power. Each ferry carries up to 47 vehicles and almost 400 crew and passengers. They transport people between the Gulf Islands and Vancouver Island.

Sailing into a truly sustainable future, the Ellen Ferry is the world's largest fully electric ferry. With zero emissions and cutting-edge battery technology, it's revolutionizing eco-friendly transportation.

BIG Breakthroughs

Electric ships too are helping to transform transportation at sea. In California, a company called Pasha Hawaii has brought in hybrid electric cargo ships to carry goods in a more environmentally friendly way. The ewolf is a hybrid-electric tugboat that is used to help large ships navigate San Diego port. It is the United States' first electric tugboat. Tugboats like this one will make navigating ports much more Earth friendly.

Overcoming Challenges

While electric ferries and ships are becoming more common, they still face engineering challenges. The batteries available to date cannot provide enough energy for the vessels to travel long distances. Most ports also do not yet have fast-charging stations for electric vehicles. However, as technology improves and more money is invested in green infrastructure, those engineering issues should be overcome.

In the future, electrical charge points in harbors could become commonplace.

Ships That Use Hydrogen

Hydrogen fuel cells are also being developed for use in ships. Like in hydrogen-powered cars, the cells convert hydrogen gas into electricity. The electricity is then used to power a motor. That drives the ship's propellers or water jets, to push the vessel forward. Excess energy created is stored in an onboard battery. It can be used later to power the ships or provide energy for other systems.

Like hydrogen-powered cars, the technology for the ships is still an issue. That is because there are few refueling stations available in the world's ports. However, just as more on-land refueling stations for cars become available in the future, the same will happen for ships. That will open up the use of these green vessels across the world's waters.

ENGINEERING SOLUTIONS

Capturing the energy of the sun may be another way that transportation across water is made more sustainable. Solar-powered boats are already in operation in some places. In India, the Aditya ferry operates in Kerala. It is fully solar-powered and can carry up to 75 passengers. Long-distance travel by solar-powered vessel could become a reality in the future, as solar-power technology improves. One solar-powered vessel, the *MS Tûranor PlanetSolar* has already completed an around-the-world voyage. That proves that ocean-wide travel on a solar-powered ship could be part of our transportation future.

Combinations of sustainable energy are being used in some projects. For example, one French ship named the *Energy Observer* is powered entirely by hydrogen, solar, and wind power.

This European ferry uses a rotor sail to power it along.

Returning to the Wind

People are turning to the wind once more to power ships. However, they are using new and improved engineering to make the most of Earth's wind. The ships have rotor sails, kite sails, and wind turbines built into their design. They also have made use of smart engineering seen in aircraft, such as Flettner fins. These are finlike structures that are positioned on a ship's hull. They are fixed on either side, normally above or below the waterline. When wind flows over the fins, it creates a lifting force. That helps power the ships forward.

Spinning Sails

Rotor sails are large cylindrical structures that spin around a central point. The sails are usually positioned on the deck or upper structure of a ship. As wind passes across the cylinder, it spins. As it spins, air on one side moves more quickly than air on the other side. The faster-moving air creates low pressure. The slower-moving air creates high pressure. The difference in pressure creates a force that moves the ship forward. Ships that have rotor sails can improve their fuel efficiency by up to 20 percent.

Kite-Flying Ships

Skysails are another engineering solution to modern sailing ships. These are sails shaped a little like kites, so they can catch the wind as a kite does. As the wind passes over them, they create lift, a little like the way an airplane wing creates lift. The kite sails are attached to the ship by a line, so that the "kite" is flown high above the ship. That allows it to capture a lot of wind. The kite is also positioned at a 45-degree angle to the ship to capture the maximum amount of wind. That helps it create a forward force that powers the ship. The additional power provided can reduce the overall fuel consumption of the ship by up to 15 percent. The ships are especially useful for making long-distance journeys across windy waters.

In the Netherlands, the Roboat is a self-driving water taxi that carries passengers along the city's canal system.

Self-Driving Ships

Some self-driving ships are being tested for both cargo and passenger transportation. These ships use AI, sensors, and automated technology. They can navigate and communicate without needing people. The Yara Birkeland is a good example of a state-of-the-art ship. It is fully self-driving and powered by battery. It was created by the Yara and Kongsberg company in Norway. It is the world's first fully electric and self-driving cargo ship and is used to transport goods between ports. The ship still operates with a crew of just three people due to regulations.

No Crew Needed

Mitsui O.S.K Lines is part of a group of Japanese organizations working on self-driving tankers. They will carry bulky goods across the world's oceans. The ships have autonomous navigation systems, sensors, and AI. They will be able to operate without a crew. The onboard systems will allow the tankers to navigate and adjust course without needing people.

Passenger Ships and Sustainable Travel

As with aircraft, long-distance passenger transportation by sea is still in its early days. However, some cruise ship companies are looking into autonomous technology. They are investigating it for navigation, avoiding collisions, and choosing the best routes. At first, these systems are likely to help crewmembers rather than replace them altogether. Along with investigating autonomous cruise ships, some companies are also exploring combining sustainable forms of power on their ships. The aim is to use a combination of fuel cells, batteries, and wind-assisted technology to power the vessels. That would make them completely emission free.

Boats That Fly

In France, the company SeaBubbles is building state-of-the-art "flying" hydrofoil boats. They can transport passengers along lakes, rivers, and urban waterways, such as canal systems. Other hydrofoil ferries are also used elsewhere in the world, to transport people quickly across short distances. Many places use them to connect islands to the mainland.

HOW IT WORKS:
A HYDROFOIL

A hydrofoil vessel has streamlined, winglike structures fitted below its hull. They are called hydrofoils. When traveling at low speed, the hull floats in the water like a traditional boat. As the vessel moves faster, water flows over and under the hydrofoils. That creates lift. When enough lift is created, the hull rises above the water surface. The vessel then avoids resistance from the water, or drag. The reduction in drag means that the vessels can move quickly across an area of water.

Hydrofoils are a smart way to move people across short stretches of water, such as lakes.

Smart ships will be able to sense other vehicles on the water.

Smarter Ways to Travel

The future looks very bright for transportation on water. Just as technology is improving navigation on land and in the air, it is helping people find their way on the water. Soon, advanced sensors on vessels will collect data that will help determine the best route to travel. That information will include weather conditions, currents at sea, and the condition of the ship or boat. Onboard predictive energy optimization systems will use all that information to control the way the vessel travels, and reduce the amount of fuel used.

Sensors for Safety

Sensors will also be able to monitor the condition of a vessel. They will check different parts such as the engine, propellers, and hull. They will alert technicians when repairs are needed. That will reduce the risk of problems occurring at sea, which will make journeys safer. It will also help to stop harmful leaks from vessels, which result in pollution of the water. For example, the risk of fuel and chemicals leaks would be detected by onboard sensor systems. Repairs could then be carried out before such harmful leaks take place.

Ships That Talk

Smart ships will also be able to communicate with each other quickly. They will use both inbuilt smart systems and external networks that connect different vessels at sea. That will allow them to communicate in real time. They will be able to know immediately what other ships or boats are traveling in the same water space. That will help them avoid collisions and make travel through busy waterways, such as ports, much easier.

Better for Passengers

Passenger experience could also be improved with new smart technology. For example, people traveling on cruise ships may be able to personalize their experience on board before their journey begins. They will be able to preprogramme their cabin temperature and lighting. They will be able to choose what entertainment to enjoy, such as movies and music. They will even be able to book services such as ordering food or onboard hairdressing and treatments ahead of their journey.

ENGINEERING SOLUTIONS

A major obstacle to making travel by water environmentally friendly is old-fashioned ports. It is possible to create ships that run on cleaner forms of energy. However, if they cannot easily refuel at ports, that makes the use of such vessels difficult. But in the future, ports should get smarter too. They will also be fitted with electric or hydrogen recharging stations. Autonomous, zero-emission tugboats will be able to work both day and night to assist ships and boats in ports. That will make the rollout of green ships around the world possible.

We are likely to see more autonomous technology in ports too. That includes autonomous cranes that lift cargo from ships and place it on lorries—without needing an operator. Drones could automatically transport goods from a port to where they are needed. They could even cover long distances over land as technology improves. All those automated services will reduce the need for human workers and speed up delivery of goods.

Future cruise ship passengers will be able to adjust their experience on board the ship using their smartphone.

THE FUTURE IS EVOLVING

The exciting thing about engineering is that the areas in which engineers work are always evolving. And there are some really exciting developments on the horizon for land, air, and water travel that will revolutionize transportation.

Helping Drivers

Advanced driver assistance systems (ADAS) are already making driving easier and safer. And future developments will make car driving even better. ADAS systems include technology that automatically adjusts the car's speed to keep a safe distance from vehicles in front. Warning systems tell the driver if they are crossing a lane line without signaling. They can also automatically steer the car back into the correct lane. Automatic braking takes place if the system detects a potential collision. That might be with another vehicle, pedestrian, or an object. If the driver becomes sleepy or shows signs of lacking focus, the system will warn them. Night-vision systems with infrared sensors also pick up pedestrians, animals, or obstacles that might not be seen with standard headlamps.

Automated systems will make car travel easier and safer.

Hyperloop systems could change the way that people commute both short and long distances.

As car technology develops, we are likely to see fully automated vehicles on the road. In-car entertainment systems, like those seen on airplanes, will also be available. Drivers will be able to sit back, relax, and watch a movie or listen to music, while their car does the driving.

Future Loop Systems

Hyperloop systems too may provide joined-up networks for all forms of transportation. They could connect travelers with airports and existing rail systems. That would provide seamless travel from one system to the other. Hyperloops may be able to take over from short- and medium-distance flight travel. They would mean flying is only required for long distances. That would provide a further solution to harmful gas emissions and the problem of global warming.

Engineers are also exploring the idea of a water-based loop system. It could carry passengers or cargo in sealed tubes underwater. Called the Sea Hyperloop, it could transport people, vehicles, and goods across bodies of water at great speed.

People Making a Difference

People are creative problem-solvers. Through smart engineering solutions, transportation has evolved from the first boats made from hollowed-out trees to advanced automated vehicles. And there are a lot more exciting ideas in the pipeline for the transportation industry, which will carry on evolving thanks to the work of brilliant engineers.

EVOLVE AS AN ENGINEER

Smart engineering solutions to the world's problems need smart brains. Without the amazing engineering minds of the past, we would never have created vehicles that helped us cross oceans, countries, and skies. Engineering is one of the most exciting fields to work in, and one of the most rewarding. If you would like to build an engineering career, explore the following pages to discover how you could work in this ever-evolving field. Perhaps one day you will help evolve our transportation future.

EVOLVING CAREERS IN ENGINEERING

There are many cutting-edge job opportunities within the transportation industry for engineers. As this rapidly changing field develops, so too do the career options within it. Here are just some of the evolving engineering roles you could explore.

Transportation Engineer

Transportation engineers plan and design roads, airports, subway systems, and other transportation systems. If you are specifically interested in transportation, this area of engineering is a great option.

Civil Engineer

If you're interested in building the infrastructure that helps transportation run, you might find civil engineering an interesting career. Civil engineers help design and construct bridges. They also plan and build roadways, tunnels, airports, waterways, and more.

Working as a transportation engineer is a fascinating job. You would help plan the design of both vehicles and the systems they use.

Aviation engineering is a rapidly growing and changing field.

Mechanical Engineer

Mechanical engineers work on machinery, equipment, and mechanical sensors. As transportation development continues to focus on "smart" solutions, mechanical engineers will be needed. They will help design and refine the equipment used on those smart roads, vehicles, and more.

Aviation and Marine Engineers

Aerospace engineers work on vehicles and systems that enable air transportation. That includes all flying vehicles and the systems that they use. Marine engineers work on the ships and vessels we use for water transportation. This includes everything from sailboats to oil tankers and aircraft carriers. They also help design and build ports and other waterways.

Materials Engineer

Materials engineers create and study different types of material. If you are interested in working on prototypes for transportation solutions, you might enjoy this field. For example, materials engineers have been heavily involved in the fields of air transportation over the years. They have developed lightweight, strong, and long-lasting materials that allow people to safely travel in the sky.

Environmental Engineer

Environmental engineers help design solutions for environmental concerns. That includes finding ways to manage and improve water pollution, air pollution, recycling, and sustainability. Virtually every type of new development requires an environmental engineer. They assess a project's impact on the environment and how it can be made more sustainable.

How to Get into Engineering

If you think some or all the roles outlined on the previous pages could be for you, the next steps in building a career in engineering start at school. Focus on STEM subjects because you will need qualifications in this area. STEM includes science, technology, engineering, and math. Engineers use math to problem solve and figure out designs, so it is an important skill to work on. Science is important too, because you'll need to understand physical science concepts such as forces, energy, and materials.

STEM Clubs and Camps

Consider joining a STEM club. This is a great place to work on your engineering skills. Many schools have clubs that focus on robotics, coding, and engineering challenges. Taking part will give you important hands-on experience that will help set you up for a career in engineering. You could also try a STEM camp. Many summer camps are STEM-focused today, to help young people develop these important skills. You can also explore the many STEM-focused online camps and classes available if you don't find an in-person one near you.

Joining a STEM club is a great way to work on your engineering knowledge.

Consider Coding and Kits

Many areas of engineering require coding skills, so working on understanding the basics of coding is a great way to get into engineering. Try platforms such as Scratch, Python, or Blockly. Programming is very important in engineering fields such as robotics and electrical engineering. You can also work on simple projects such as games, apps, and easy robots to put what you have learned into practice. Having fun with kits can also help build your engineering skills. Try working with LEGO™, Arduino, and similar kits to build robots, electronic devices, and gadgets.

Any practical work like this will fire up your engineering brain and show you how exciting this area can be.

Talk to Other Engineers

Tell your teachers that you are interested in engineering, and they may be able to put you in touch with engineers who could talk to you about career options. You may even be able to visit engineers at work and see what a day in the life in this career is like. School counselors are also great people to talk to about career options, and they may be able to find engineering mentors for you to talk to. They will also be able to advise on courses to take once you finish school that will help put you on your path to a career in engineering.

Find Out More

When thinking about the next steps after school, spend time researching engineering programs at colleges and universities. The more you can find out now, the better placed you will be when the time comes to apply for a course.

There are different types of engineering, like mechanical, electrical, civil, aerospace, and environmental engineering. Each one leads to different kinds of jobs, so exploring your options early can help you decide what interests you most. Many colleges offer open days, online tours, and information sessions so you can see what their programs are like and ask questions.

GLOSSARY

adapt to make something suitable for a new use or purpose

aerodynamic able to move through the air

air resistance the force acting on an object that is moving through air flowing in the opposite direction

algorithm a set of rules to be followed when making calculations or problem-solving

altitudes heights above sea level

artificial intelligence (AI) software that performs tasks that normally require human intelligence

atmosphere the protective layers of gas that surround Earth

automobile a motor vehicle with wheels that is used to transport people

bow the front part of a ship or boat

byproduct a secondary product made as a result of making an initial product

canals humanmade waterways that allow boats and ships to travel between bodies of water

carrier companies businesses that offer transportation services

cement a chemical substance that acts as a binder, for example, to bind sand and gravel together. Cement hardens and sets

center of gravity a point from which the weight of a body or system acts

chain drive a mechanical system that uses a chain and sprockets to transmit power between two paths

chariots two-wheeled vehicles drawn by horses

circuit a closed path that allows electricity, data, or signals to flow through it

civilizations societies that have a particular culture and way of life

climate change a change in climate patterns

commercial related to the intention of making a profit

congested crowded with traffic or people so that it's difficult to move through

consumption using something

controlled remotely operated from a distance, using radio or electrical signals

crew a group of people who work on and operate a ship, aircraft, or other vehicle

currents the parts of a fluid body, such as air and water, that move continuously in a certain direction

cylindrical having straight parallel sides and a circular or oval shape

data information

deck the floor of a ship

diesel a fuel designed for use in a diesel engine

driver-assisted systems technology that helps drivers operate their vehicles

electric charge port a point at which an electric vehicle is connected to a charging station

electric current the flow of charged particles moving through an electric conductor

electromagnetic waves a form of radiation that travels through an electromagnetic field

emissions substances released into the air

emits gives off

energy the ability to do work

engines machines designed to convert forms of energy into mechanical energy

environment the surroundings or conditions in which a person, animal, or plant lives

evolved developed gradually from a simple to a more complex form

facial recognition a way of identifying a person using an image of their face

ferries boats that transport passengers, cargo, and vehicles across bodies of water

force a power that causes an object to move or that changes movement

fossil fuel an energy source, including coal, oil, and natural gas, that was formed when prehistoric plants and animals died and were buried by layers of rock. Fossil fuels are nonrenewable

freight trains railway trains that carry cargo rather than people

gear a toothed wheel that works with others to alter the speed of a vehicle

gliders aircraft that have long, fixed wings and no engines. They fly by gliding

global positioning system (GPS) a navigation system that uses satellites in space

global warming the overall increase in the temperature of Earth's atmosphere, which scientists believe is increasing due to greenhouse gas emissions

greenhouse gases gases such as carbon dioxide that contribute to the warming of Earth's atmosphere

grid the network of power plants, transmission lines, substations, and distribution lines, that deliver electricity from power stations to homes and businesses

Hittites an ancient people who lived in what is now Turkey, Syria, and Iraq

hull the main body of a ship or other vessel including the bottom, sides, and deck

hydrofoil boats that use winglike structures to lift their hull out of the water

hydrogen balloon a balloon filled with hydrogen gas. Hydrogen is lighter than air so the balloon rises in the air

hydrogen fuel cell a device that uses hydrogen to produce electricity, heat, and water

Industrial Revolution a period of major economic and technological change that began in the eighteenth century in Europe and then spread to North America

infrared sensors sensors that operate by detecting infrared radiation

innovations new methods, ideas, or products

internal-combustion engine an engine that burns fuel and air to create power

iron ore rocks and minerals from which metallic iron can be extracted, or taken out

laser pulses bursts of light created by a laser

LED an abbreviation for light-emitting diode, which is a device that gives off light when an electric current flows through it.

LiDAR a remote-sensing technology that uses lasers to create three-dimensional (3-D) models of Earth's surface

lift a force that acts on an aircraft to lift it upward

locks enclosed chambers in a canal with gates at each end. Locks enable vehicles to be raised or lowered by adding or releasing water

machine learning a type of AI that allows computers to learn from data and improve their performance over time

Mesopotamians an ancient civilization that existed in what is now Iraq between 600 and 400 BCE

Middle Ages a period in European history that lasted from the fifth century to the fifteenth century

mines places where minerals, metals, and other materials are extracted, or taken out of the earth

molecules groups of atoms bonded together
motor a machine that produces motion or power for doing work
navigation a way of finding direction from one place to another
pedestrian a person walking from one place to another
Phoenicians an ancient civilization that existed between 3000 and 50 BCE in the Phoenician city-states in what would today be Lebanon and parts of Syria and Israel
pistons a device that transfers heat energy into a mechanical energy
pitch the up-and-down motion of an aircraft's nose or how the aircraft moves around its side-to-side axis
pollution harmful substances
power outages breaks in the supply of power such as electricity, often caused by storms
predict to forecast what is likely to happen
pressure the force exerted on or against an object by something in contact with it
pressurized to put something under a pressure
prototype the first versions or devices from which others are developed
puncture-resistant is not easily punctured
radar a system for detecting the presence, direction, distance, and speed of objects. Radar works by sending out pulses of radio waves which reflect off the surface of objects, thereby providing information about them
ram a weapon found on the front of a ship and used to hit enemy ships
real-time information information that is available as soon as it's generated
remote far away
robots machines that can do specific tasks with little or no human intervention
roll the side-to-side motion of an aircraft's wings, or the rocking back and forth of a plane
rotors the turning parts of an electrical machine
rural related to the countryside
sea level the average height of the ocean's surface
sensors devices that detect or measure things in the environment
software computer programs
solar panels devices that convert sunlight into electricity
solar-powered powered by solar energy
stabilization making something physically more secure or stable
stirrups frames or rings that hold the foot of a horse rider in place. The stirrup is attached to the saddle by a strap
suspension systems the systems that stabilize a vehicle and control how it handles bumps and dips in the road
sustainable able to be maintained at a certain rate or level
technicians skilled professionals who work in a technical field
terrain land
thrust the force that propels an engine forward
titanium alloys metals made from titanium mixed with other elements, such as aluminum
vessels ships and boats
water vapor water that has turned into a gas
wind turbines devices that convert the kinetic energy of wind into electrical energy
yaw a side-to-side movement

FIND OUT MORE

Books

DK. *Transport!* (Knowledge Encyclopedia). DK Children, 2024.

Lake. J. *The Evolution of Transportation Technology* (Evolving Technology). Rosen Publishing Group, 2019.

Small, Cathleen. *How to Choose Your Perfect Engineering Career* (STEM Career Choices). Cheriton Children's Books, 2023.

Websites

Find out more about transportation and its history at:
https://kids.britannica.com/students/article/transportation/277414

Find a useful and informative timeline for transportation and energy use from the Industrial Revolution to modern times at:
www.eia.gov/kids/history-of-energy/timelines/transportation.php

Learn more about the transportation revolution in the United States at:
https://mlpp.pressbooks.pub/americanenvironmentalhistory/chapter/chapter-6-transportation-revolution

Publisher's note to educators and parents:
All the websites featured above have been carefully reviewed to ensure that they are suitable for students. However, many websites change often, and we cannot guarantee that a site's future contents will continue to meet our high standards of educational value. Please be advised that students should be closely monitored whenever they access the Internet.

INDEX

ABOUT THE AUTHORS

Sarah Eason and Cathleen Small have written a wide variety of books for teens, including many STEM titles.